3-D GRAPHIC Organizers

20 Innovative, Easy-to-Make Learning Tools
That Reinforce Key Concepts and Motivate All Students!

Daniel J. Barnekow

New York • Toronto • London • Auckland • Sydney
Mexico City • New Delhi • Hong Kong • Buenos Aires

Teaching
Resources

For My Girls—Meg and Kate

Editor: Mela Ottaiano
Cover and interior design: Maria Lilja
ISBN-13: 978-0-545-00520-3
ISBN-10: 0-545-00520-5

2 3 4 5 6 7 8 9 10   40   15 14 13 12 11 10 09

Contents

Introduction...4

3-D Graphic Organizers (With Suggested Topics for Sample Projects)

11-Flap Flip Table
(Math: Memorizing the
Multiplication Tables) 10

7-Flap Flip Table
(Social Studies: Asking and
Answering Questions About
a Historical Event).............................12

Triptych
(Science: Describing a Landform) 15

Flip Chart
(Science: Identifying the
Characteristics of Life) 17

Folded List Maker
(Social Studies: Parts of a Map) 20

Idea Box
(Science: Describing a Habitat) 22

Mini-Book
(Reading/Language Arts:
Summarizing a Book or Story) 24

Object Pop-Up
(Reading/Language Arts: Learning
and Presenting Punctuation Rules)....28

Person Pop-Up
(Social Studies: Studying a Well-Known
Historical Figure) 31

Right Triangle
(Math: Explaining the Pythagorean
Theorem)...34

Triple Flap
(Science: Comparing the Three
Types of Rocks)..................................37

3-D Boat
(Social Studies: Studying
an Explorer)......................................40

Mini-Accordion
(Social Studies: Creating a Timeline).. 42

Spinning Wheel
(Math: Fractions, Decimals,
and Percents) 45

Slide Chart
(Science: Classifying Living Things) ... 49

Twist Tube
(Math: Understanding Place
Values) 52

Double Twist Tube
(Reading/Language Arts: Identifying
Synonyms and Antonyms) 55

Bookmark
(Reading/Language Arts: Learning
New Words While Reading) 58

Mobile 1
(Reading/Language Arts:
Studying a Part of Speech)................60

Mobile 2
(Math: Learning the Flat Shapes)......62

All reproducible templates are available on the companion CD.

Introduction

3-D Graphic Organizers brings a whole new dimension to a powerful learning tool. Students will have fun constructing and manipulating three-dimensional organizers, and they are rewarded with a more enjoyable lesson, a tangible outcome, and a greater sense of accomplishment.

A Proven Teaching Tool

This 3-D approach builds on the foundation laid by the more familiar two-dimensional graphic organizers, which have long been recognized as one of the most reliable of all teaching tools. Scores of studies have demonstrated their usefulness in nearly every teaching situation. They have been proven helpful across grade levels, in all subject areas, throughout the teaching cycle, and with students of different learning styles and abilities. Hard measures of student performance always improve when graphic organizers are integrated into the curriculum. According to researchers at the Department of Education, "There is solid evidence for the effectiveness of graphic organizers in facilitating learning."

Benefits of 3-D Graphic Organizers

You'll quickly recognize the benefits of using 3-D graphic organizers with your students. They work extremely well not only with visual learners, like their two-dimensional counterparts, but with kinesthetic learners as well. The acts of making and manipulating the organizers focus students and help them retain more information. In addition, students take pride in having successfully constructed something, and these positive feelings are highly correlated with learning. The finished models are particularly suitable for display in the classroom and at home, and they serve as powerful reminders, reference tools, and reinforcement agents. Parents, too, appreciate these projects as concise, easy-to-understand evidence of what their children are studying, learning, and accomplishing in school.

The fun, interactive activities in this book give students a break from their routine, yet focus them on essential knowledge. Rich in possibilities for individual, small-group, and whole-class learning, these organizers truly help your students "build" their knowledge.

The 3-D Graphic Organizers

This resource provides templates and instructions for creating 20 different 3-D graphic organizers. These organizers meet the following criteria:

* **Pedagogically sound:** They help teachers teach and students learn.

* **Easily constructed:** Students can build them with limited assistance.

* **Simple:** They are not so complicated that they interfere with learning.

* **Fun:** Students love them!

* **Flexible:** Most of them can be used with many different topics across the curriculum.

The sample projects have been evenly divided across the content areas—reading and language arts, social studies, math, and science. They cover a broad range of topics from learning punctuation rules to identifying the parts of a map, from describing a landform to understanding place value. There are also suggestions for using various 3-D graphic organizers to target vital research, study, and critical-thinking skills. Again, the organizers are flexible, so feel free to use them in any way you or students think best suits their learning needs.

For each organizer, you will find a general description of its best use and key objectives, a materials list, step-by-step assembly instructions, and a template that all correspond with a picture of a completed project. Also included are ideas for extending the lesson and other topics for which the organizer is well suited.

Once you select and introduce the activity, simply distribute photocopies of the template and have students assemble it by cutting, folding, and taping.

You can use each project as an introductory activity, a component of a core lesson, a fun review, a way to extend learning, and even an assessment. To assess a completed graphic organizer, use the simple rubric on page 9.

Building 3-D Graphic Organizers

Most students will be able to complete the 3-D graphic organizers on their own. However, the majority of the organizers require the use of scissors, a few require staples, and one requires a brad, so close supervision is necessary. Generally, constructing a 3-D graphic organizer consists of three steps:

1. Photocopy and distribute the template.

2. Students cut where necessary.

3. Students fold and tape (or staple) where necessary.

After the organizer has been constructed, students can complete it by writing down appropriate information, illustrating it, and so on. (In a few cases, where indicated, the 3-D organizers must be filled in and illustrated before they are assembled.)

Because they are simple by design, the assembly of most of the 3-D graphic organizers is self-evident. However, use photos of the completed samples as a guide, when necessary.

Symbols on the Templates

Symbols on the templates will guide you and your students while assembling the organizers.

_____	Solid lines should be cut.
✂	A scissors icon reinforces the idea of cutting along the solid lines.
- - - -	Dashed lines should be folded.
Project	Project requires paper to be oriented vertically.
Project	Project requires paper to be oriented horizontally.

Materials

The 3-D graphic organizers are designed to work with standard copier paper. However, copying the templates onto a slightly heavier paper will add to their longevity, and using colored paper on occasion will make them more appealing to students.

Most of the organizers need only scissors and tape to construct and a pen or pencil to complete. A few require additional common items. Here is a comprehensive list of materials:

* scissors
* tape
* double-sided tape
* stapler

* straightedge
* colored pencils
* colored markers
* string

* brads
* hole punch

How to Use the Companion CD

The companion CD is a flexible tool that will help simplify your teaching. It contains customizable versions of all the templates shown in this book, which are also available as traditional reproducible pages. Simply photocopy a graphic organizer template or, if you don't have immediate access to a photocopier, just print multiple copies from the CD. You may fill in the digital form—typing in notes and prompts before printing to create different assignments or scaffold learning—and save the digital file to update in the future. In fact, you may want to make a folder on a classroom hard drive for each student. This way, if students are more comfortable typing in their responses, they will be able to have easy access to edit and polish their organizer.

The customizable fields will be indicated by highlighting on screen. Note: You must check the "Highlight fields" box to view the highlighted customizable sections. The highlighting will not appear on the printouts. In addition, while previewing the files you will notice that not all fields on the templates are customizable. However, to keep a consistent look in a graphic organizer, you or students may want to type out information in a separate document using the standard Times New Roman font and 12 point size. Then, print out, cut apart, and tape (or glue) in the appropriate area.

Tips!

* To customize and save the files on the CD, you will need to use Adobe Reader™, version 7.0 or higher. You can find a download that is available free of charge for Mac and PC systems at www. adobe.com/products/ acrobat/readstep2.

* Use the Tab key to move between the customizable fields, or click directly on a particular field.

* Type a title or other heading in capital letters to make it stand out.

Here are some examples of prompts across the curriculum you might use for the Triptych 3-D graphic organizer:

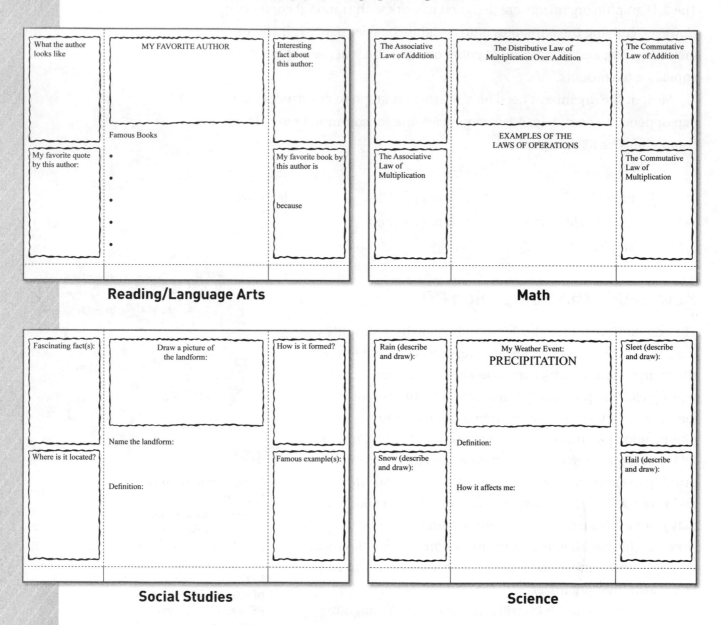

Reading/Language Arts

Math

Social Studies

Science

Enjoying 3-D Graphic Organizers

Above all, these organizers should be fun for you and your students to use. If you ask what adults remember from their elementary school days, most will mention making something. Our hope is that one of the 3-D graphic organizers from this book will help you give your students similarly fond memories.

Assessment Rubric

LEVEL	DESCRIPTION
5	**Excellent Work:** 3-D graphic organizer is constructed correctly; information is complete; information is accurate; information is presented logically; extra effort apparent in neatness, decoration, and so on.
4	**Very Good Work:** 3-D graphic organizer is constructed correctly; information is complete; information is accurate; information is presented logically.
3	**Good Work:** 3-D graphic organizer is constructed correctly; most information is accurate; most information is presented logically.
2	**Good Effort:** 3-D graphic organizer may or may not be constructed correctly; some information is missing; some information is inaccurate; some information is presented illogically.
1	**Little Effort:** 3-D graphic organizer is not constructed correctly; most information is missing; most information is inaccurate; most information is presented illogically.

11-Flap Flip Table

This 3-D graphic organizer helps students record, study, and memorize key facts.

Objectives

* Express the multiplication tables from the 1s through the 10s.
* Memorize the multiplication tables from the 1s through the 10s.

Time Required

* about 60 minutes

Materials

* 11-Flap Flip Table Template (page 11)
* scissors

Introduce

Explain to students that multiplication is the same as adding a given number of groups of the same size. The number sentence "3 x 4" means the same as adding together 3 groups of 4 (or 4 groups of 3).

What to Do

1. Distribute the template to students and guide them in its construction.
2. Direct students to write "The 1s" on the top flap and to write the 1s multiplication facts on the following 10 flaps (1 x 1, 1 x 2, 1 x 3 . . . 1 x 10). They should write the answer to each equation under each flap.
3. Repeat the process for the other multiplication facts (the 2s, the 3s, and so on).

Extend

Have students quiz each other on their multiplication. Have them multiply fun things such as the number of pets or siblings each has, their respective ages, or the number of blueberries they can eat at one time.

Ways to Use Across the Curriculum

* **Reading/Language Arts:** Distinguish the parts of speech; distinguish punctuation marks.
* **Social Studies:** Detail facts about a community, state, or country.
* **Science:** List steps in the scientific method; define scientific terms.
* **Study Skills:** Take notes; learn Dewey Decimal System classes; create a homework checklist.

How to Construct

1. Cut out the template and the flaps, along the solid lines.
2. Fold left to right, along the dashed lines. Make sure flaps are on the left and fold over the solid piece.
3. Be sure the organizer is oriented vertically.
4. Fold up the ends of the flaps into small tabs, which make the flaps easier to grasp.
5. Fill in the important information.

Project

7-Flap Flip Table

Social Studies: Asking and Answering
Questions About a Historical Event

This 3-D graphic organizer
helps students record, study,
and memorize key facts.

Objectives

* Formulate questions about
  a historical event.
* Explore an important event in detail.

Time Required

* about 90 minutes in addition
  to research time

Materials

* 7-Flap Flip Table Template (page 14)
* scissors

Introduce

Challenge students to identify "question words." Record
their responses on the board. Continue until they have
identified the six question words: *who, what, where,
when, why,* and *how.* Explain how asking and answering
questions that begin with each of these words will help
them fully understand historical events. Provide an
example from your current instruction.

What to Do

1. Assign a particular historical event (or events) for
   students to investigate.

2. Distribute the template to students and guide them in
   its construction.

3. Direct students to write the name of the historical
   event on the top flap and to create questions about the
   event that begin with each of the six question words on
   the remaining flaps. Ensure the appropriateness of the questions.

4. Have students exchange graphic organizers with a partner and answer
   the questions, or have them answer their own questions.

5. Ask students to write a brief description of the event or an illustration
   of it under the top flap.

How to Construct

1. Cut out the template
   and the flaps, along
   the solid lines.

2. Fold left to right, along
   the dashed lines. Make
   sure flaps are on the
   left and fold over the
   solid piece.

3. Be sure the organizer
   is oriented vertically.

4. Fold up the ends of the
   flaps into small tabs,
   which make the flaps
   easier to grasp.

5. Fill in the important
   information.

Extend

Create a classroom game in which students challenge each other to answer the questions and award points for correct responses.

Ways to Use Across the Curriculum

* **Language Arts:** Ask and answer questions about a piece of literature or an author; record the names and traits of characters in a work of fiction; list the names of authors and their works.
* **Math:** Name very large numbers and correctly identify their value; recognize and identify the value of American coins; record mathematical symbols and their meanings; sketch flat shapes and their names.
* **Science:** List in order and describe the colors of the spectrum; ask and answer questions about a scientist or a science topic; list and describe the steps in the scientific method; list body systems and their functions.
* **Study Skills:** Take notes; create a sequenced to-do list for keeping up with homework.

7-Flap Flip Table Template

Project

Project

3-D Graphic Organizers © 2009 by Daniel J. Barnekow, Scholastic Inc. • page 14

Triptych

This 3-D graphic organizer helps students identify and describe different elements of a topic and present what they learn to others.

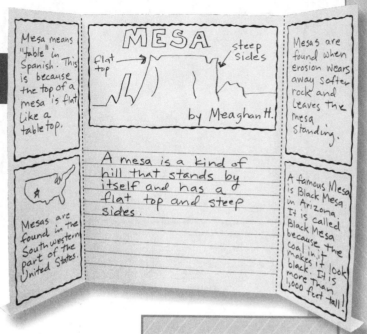

Objectives

* Describe a landform.
* Identify a selected landform's key characteristics.
* Discuss how people interact with a landform.

Time Required

* about 60 minutes

Materials

* Triptych Template (page 16)
* scissors

Introduce

Ensure students understand what landforms are (distinct features of the Earth's surface, such as mountains, valleys, and dunes) and invite them to name some well-known examples—the Grand Canyon, for example— and some notable local ones.

What to Do

1. Create a list of landforms and assign one to each student.
2. Distribute the template to students and guide them in its construction.
3. Direct students to write the name of their landform in the center box and then complete their organizer with appropriate information and illustrations. Suggestions: definition of the landform, description of the landform, where the landform occurs, how the landform is formed, same famous examples of the landform, why the landform is important to people.

How to Construct

1. Cut out the template along the solid lines.
2. Turn template horizontally and fill in the important information.
3. Cut along the two short lines at the bottom of the organizer and fold back the three tabs to create "feet."
4. Fold in and crease the two side panels. Then open them somewhat so the organizer will stand up.

Extend

Have students make a simple model of their chosen landform and present it, surrounded by the three sides of the Triptych.

Ways to Use Across the Curriculum

* **Reading/Language Arts:** Describe the life or list the work of a famous writer; put together a mini book report.
* **Math:** Identify and give examples of the laws of operations.
* **Science:** Describe the life of a famous scientist; detail information about an invention or a scientific discovery; show examples of different weather events.

Triptych Template

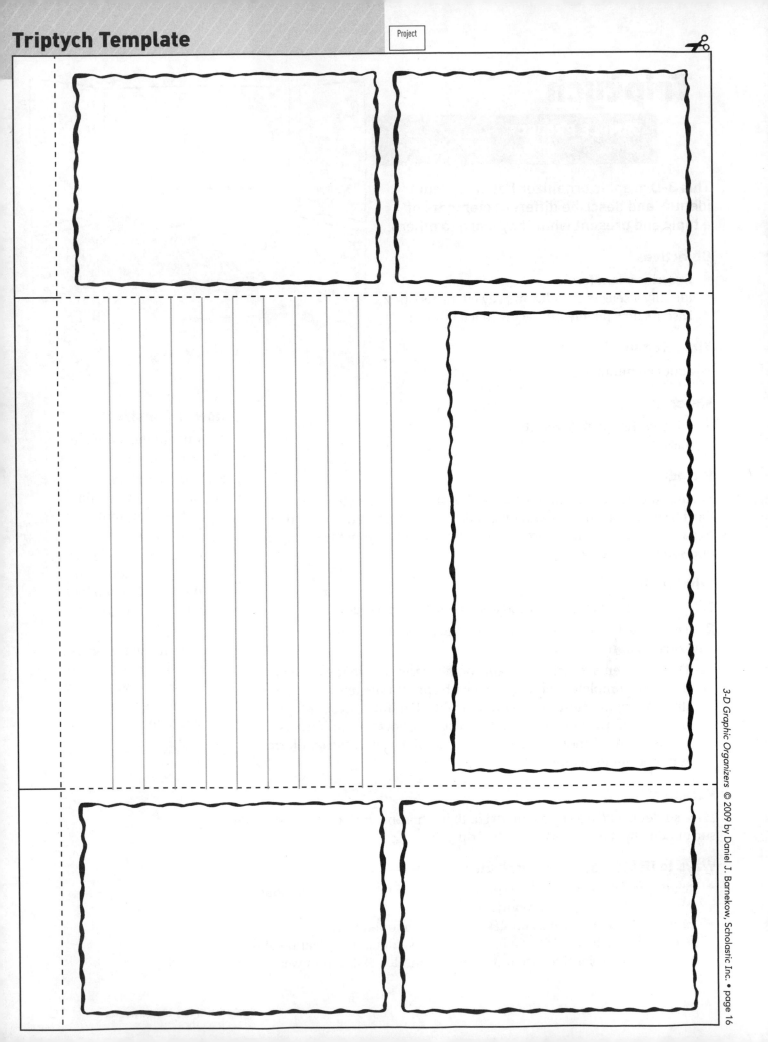

3-D Graphic Organizers © 2009 by Daniel J. Barnekow, Scholastic Inc. • page 16

Flip Chart

This 3-D graphic organizer helps students identify and record key characteristics of an object, an event, or a concept.

Objectives

* List the characteristics shared by all living organisms (reproduction, growth, metabolism, movement, responsiveness, adaptation).
* Explain why each characteristic is included in the list.

Time Required

* about 45 minutes

Materials

* Flip Chart Template (1 copy of page 18 and 2 copies of page 19)
* stapler

Introduce

Ask students what makes something "alive." Challenge them to explain, for example, why a cloud is not considered to be a living thing.

What to Do

1. Distribute the template to students and guide them in its construction.
2. Have students label the top flap "The Characteristics of Life."
3. Direct students to label each flap with one of the characteristics of life and a brief discussion about it.
4. Students may also color and illustrate each flap.

Extend

Discuss viruses with the class and why they fall short of being true living things (viruses cannot reproduce on their own).

Ways to Use Across the Curriculum

* **Reading/Language Arts:** Keep track of main characters in a book.
* **Math:** Identify and practice the order of operations.
* **Social Studies:** Identify facts about a community, state, or country.
* **Study Skills:** Create self-quizzes.

How to Construct

1. Cut out the templates along the solid lines.
2. Fold each page, as indicated.
3. Stagger the folded pages.
4. Be sure they are aligned and crease folds again tightly.
5. Staple twice at crease.
6. Fill in important information.

Flip Chart Template

Project

fold back and turn page over (top back page 1)

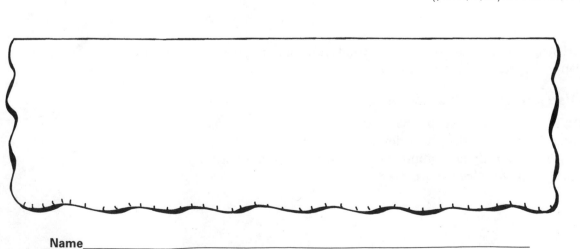

Name_____

fold back and turn page over (top back page 2)

fold back and turn page over (top back page 3)

Folded List Maker

This 3-D graphic organizer helps students identify and study key elements of a topic or concept.

Objectives
* Identify the major parts of a map.
* Describe how to read a map properly.

Time Required
* about 45 minutes

Materials
* Folded List Maker Template (page 21)
* scissors

Introduce
Invite students to name as many places as possible where they see maps (in cars, in train or bus stations, at shopping centers, on television, etc.). Point out that maps are so common because they are so helpful, and that there are key elements to look for while reading maps.

How to Construct
1. Cut out the template and the flaps, along the solid lines.
2. Fold left to right, along the dashed line.
3. Be sure the organizer is oriented vertically.
4. Fill in the important information.

What to Do
1. Distribute the template to students and guide them in its construction.
2. Direct students to lift the flaps and write a key element underneath each one, in the following order: map title, key or legend, scale, compass rose, labels.
3. On top of each flap, students should draw a sketch or create an icon that represents the element.
4. Finally, to the right of each flap, students should write a definition or description of the element.
5. Point out that understanding the key elements of a map—and looking for them in the order they're listed on their graphic organizers—will help them get the most from a map.

Extend
Have student pairs work on memorizing both the elements of a map and the order in which they should be considered.

Ways to Use Across the Curriculum
* **Reading/Language Arts:** Create a spelling or vocabulary words lists; identify commonly misused or misspelled words.
* **Math:** Record arithmetic rules; list geometric formulas and show examples.
* **Science:** Detail the contributions of a scientist.
* **Study Skills:** Generate a project checklist; create self-quizzes.

Folded List Maker Template

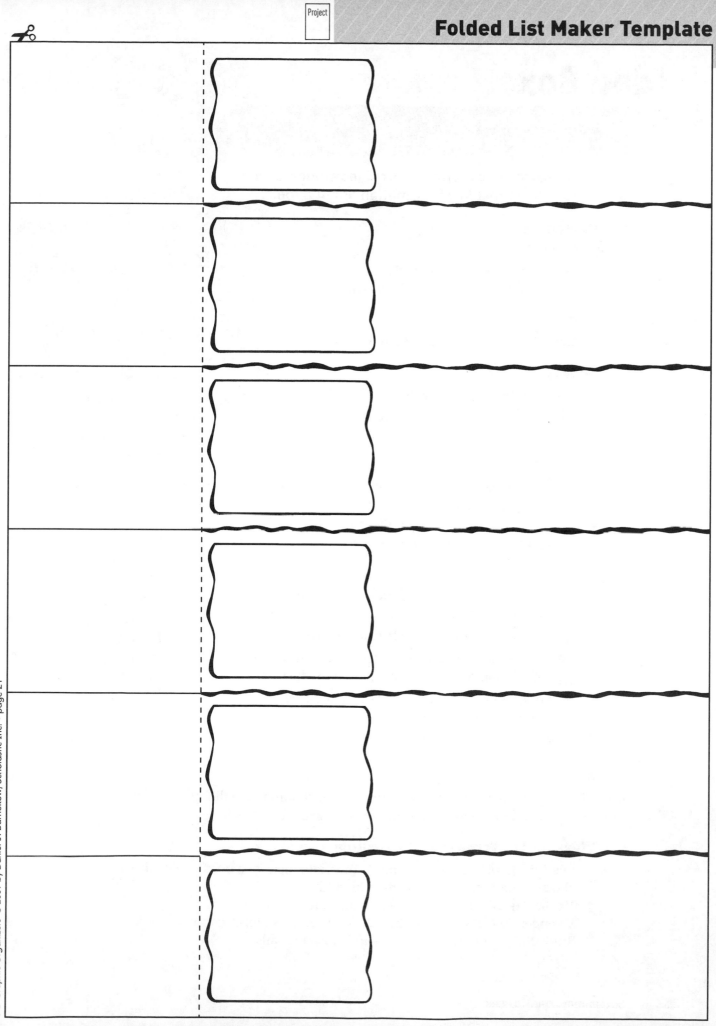

Idea Box

This 3-D graphic organizer provides students with a place to collect key information about a topic.

Objectives

* Define *habitat*.
* Investigate a selected habitat.
* Identify the key elements of a selected habitat.

Time Required

* about 75 minutes in addition to research time

Materials

* Idea Box Template (page 23)
* scissors
* tape

Introduce

Ask students to share the names of any habitats they have heard of. Provide simple examples, such as the forest and the ocean, and segue into a discussion of different habitats and the creatures that live in them.

What to Do

1. Assign specific habitats to students, or let them choose one they'd like to study.
2. Direct students to conduct research on their habitat.
3. Distribute the template to students. Then have them list the characteristics of their habitat on the inserts.
4. Have students label and decorate their boxes appropriately (before assembly).
5. Guide them in its construction.

How to Construct

1. Cut out box template and the inserts, along the solid lines.
2. Cut out slot in top of box.
3. Label and decorate the box.
4. Fold as indicated.
5. Tape box together. Do not tape lid.
6. Use the inserts to record important information to store in the box.

Extend

Challenge students to find common elements among the different ecosystems and explain how their ecosystems overlap with each other.

Ways to Use Across the Curriculum

* **Reading/Language Arts:** Compile the main ideas of a book; collect key facts about a character; brainstorm writing ideas.
* **Math:** Describe characteristics of flat shapes.
* **Science:** Collect key facts about a community, state, or country.
* **Study Skills:** Identify main idea and collect details.

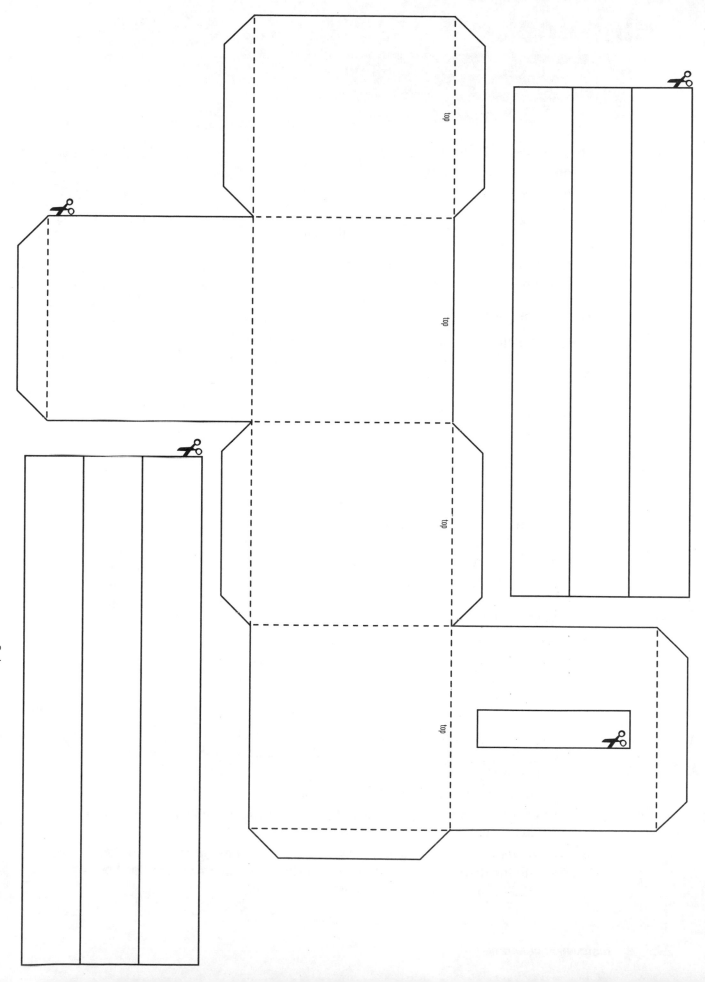

top

top

top

top

Mini-Book

This 3-D graphic organizer helps students summarize information.

Objectives

* Understand summary as a concept.
* Identify main ideas and details.
* Develop summarizing skills.

Time Required

* about 60 minutes

Materials

* Mini-Book Template (1 copy of page 26 and at least 1 copy of page 27)
* scissors
* stapler

Introduce

Invite a student to "tell about" a recent event (e.g., what happened on the playground, in class yesterday, or on a television show). Explain to the class how the student summarized by highlighting the main events or ideas.

What to Do

1. Assign students books or stories to summarize.

2. Distribute the template to students and guide them in its construction.

3. Have students write the title of the book or story they are summarizing on the cover of the mini-book. Then direct them to write a sentence or sentence fragment on each page or pair of pages in the mini-book. Each sentence or sentence fragment should describe a main event or idea of the book or story.

4. Students may illustrate each page or spread as appropriate. Emphasize that just as their mini-books are smaller versions of the originals, so their summaries should be smaller versions of the narratives.

5. For longer works, students may include additional template pages before assembling their mini-books or divide the book among multiple mini-books.

How to Construct

1. Cut each template page, first along the outer edges, and then in half along the center solid line.

2. Stack the mini-book pages so the front and back covers are on the top.

3. Fold into a book.

4. Use two staples to bind the book on the spine.

Extend

Have students who summarized the same work compare and contrast their mini-books. Discuss with the class the value of summarizing as a comprehension strategy.

Ways to Use Across the Curriculum

* **Math:** Keep a log of formulas or rules.
* **Social Studies:** Write a mini-biography.
* **Science:** Write a mini-book about the seasons; summarize a science textbook chapter.
* **Study Skills:** Record field notes.

Mini-Book Template

By _____

back cover

front cover

Mini-Book Template

Object Pop-Up

This 3-D graphic organizer helps students organize and present important information about an object or concept.

Objectives

* Identify punctuation marks.
* Describe proper usage of punctuation marks.

Time Required

* about 75 minutes

Materials

* Object Pop-Up Template (page 30)
* scissors
* tape

Introduce

Name and discuss the different punctuation marks that students often see while they are reading. Invite students to tell you the symbol associated with each mark.

.	period
?	question mark
!	exclamation point
" "	quotation marks
:	colon
;	semicolon
—	dash
( )	parentheses
[ ]	brackets
,	comma
-	hyphen
'	apostrophe

How to Construct

1. Cut out large rectangle and two smaller pieces, as indicated.
2. Fold large rectangle 90 degrees.
3. Fold the hinge as indicated.
4. Attach the hinge to the large rectangle with tape.
5. Use the pop-up piece to create the punctuation mark and tape it to the hinge.
6. Fold rectangle down. Ensure that internal pieces fold properly. Crease the fold.
7. Fill in the important information.

What to Do

1. Assign specific punctuation marks to each student or small group of students.

2. Distribute the template to students and guide them in its construction.

3. Have students draw their assigned punctuation mark on the pop-up piece.

4. Tell the students to write the name of their punctuation mark in large letters at the top of the vertical flap and to record the common rules for its use on the horizontal flap.

Extend

Have students exchange organizers with a partner and quiz one another on the rules of punctuation or how to apply them. Have students exchange organizers with different partners so they get as much exposure to as many punctuation marks as possible.

Ways to Use Across the Curriculum

* **Math:** Learn math symbols.
* **Social Studies:** Describe the benefits of a famous invention; describe the characteristics or significance of a famous place.
* **Science:** Create a mini report about a planet or other element of the solar system; detail key information about an animal.
* **Study Skills:** Identify a main idea and supporting details.

Object Pop-Up Template

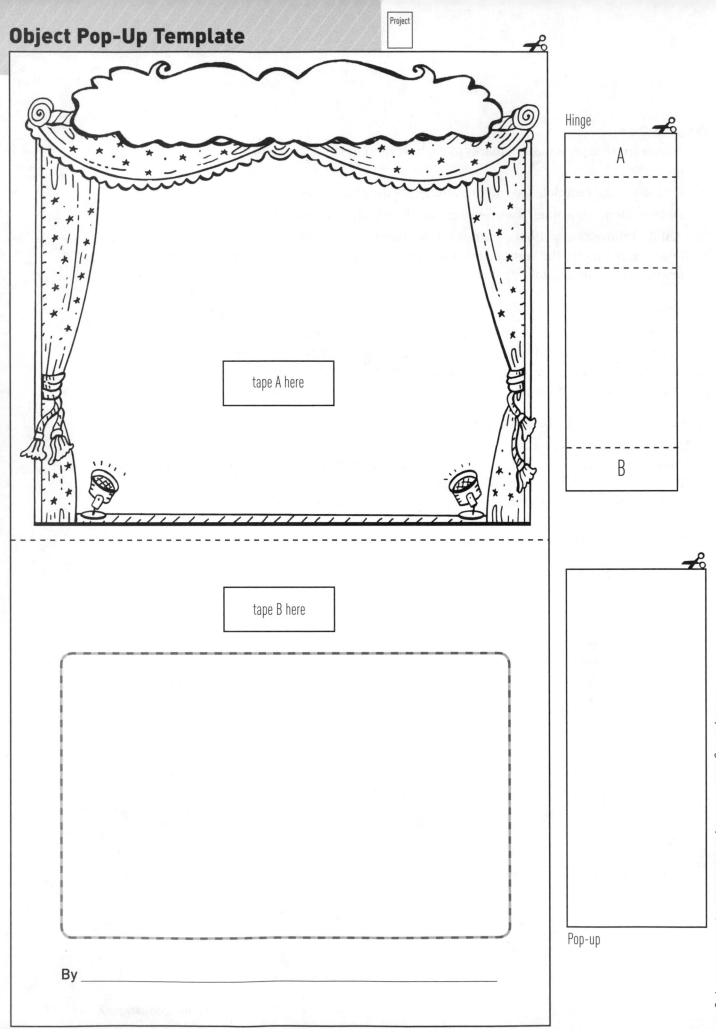

tape A here

Hinge

A

B

tape B here

By _____

Pop-up

Person Pop-Up

This 3-D graphic organizer helps students to organize and present information about a person.

Objectives

* Formulate questions about a historical figure.
* Conduct biographical research.
* Present information gleaned from research.

Time Required

* about 90 minutes in addition to research time

Materials

* Person Pop-Up Template (page 33)
* scissors
* tape

Introduce

Invite students to name famous people, either from another era or today. Choose one, and challenge students to identify the facts about this person they would tell someone who had never heard of him or her. List some categories on the board (what the person accomplished, when he or she lived, and so on). Tell students they will find out these facts about an important person in history.

What to Do

1. Assign particular historical figures for students to research, or assist them in making their own choices.

2. Distribute the template to students and guide them in its construction.

3. Direct students to complete the graphic organizer by writing the name of the historical figure in large letters on the vertical flap, coloring the pop-up figure appropriately, and writing important information about the person on both the vertical and horizontal flaps.

Nellie Bly

Time/Place
Born: May 5, 1864, in Pennsylvania; Died: January 27, 19__ in New York.

Personality Traits
adventurous, determined, bold, creative, caring

Quote
"If you want __ do it, you ca__ it. The quest__ is, do you wa__ to do it?"

Occupation
journalist, author, world traveler

Nellie Bly was a reporter. She would go undercover to learn about different places and write about them for newspapers. One time, she pretended to be a criminal to see how the police treated women. She is also famous for taking an amazing journey around the whole world in 72 days. Nellie Bly did these things in a time when women were not even supposed to have jobs! In fact, she had to use a fake name on her newspaper stories. Her real name was Elizabeth Cochrane.

By Kate B.

How to Construct

1. Cut out large rectangle and two smaller pieces, as indicated.

2. Fold large rectangle 90 degrees.

3. Fold the hinge as indicated.

4. Attach the hinge to the large rectangle with tape.

5. Use the pop-up piece to create the person and tape it to the hinge.

6. Fold rectangle down. Ensure that internal pieces fold properly. Crease the fold.

7. Fill in the important information.

Extend

Have students use their completed graphic organizers to introduce their historical figure to the class. Arrange students' completed graphic organizers in a tabletop display.

Ways to Use Across the Curriculum

* **Reading/Language Arts:** Report on a famous author; present information about an important literary character.
* **Math:** Report on an important mathematician.
* **Science:** Report on a famous scientist.
* **Study Skills:** Reflect on own academic strengths and areas to work on.

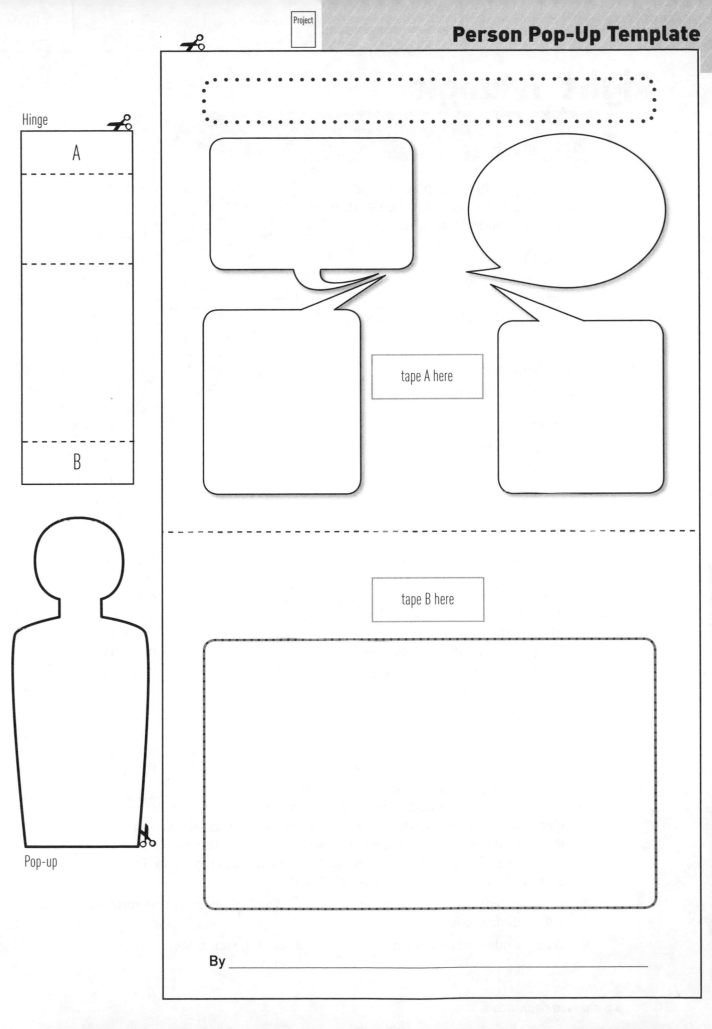

Hinge

A

B

Pop-up

tape A here

tape B here

By _____

Right Triangle

This 3-D graphic organizer helps students understand and remember the Pythagorean theorem.

Objectives

* Identify the characteristics of right triangles.
* Explain and apply the Pythagorean theorem.

Time Required

* about 30 minutes

Materials

* Right Triangle Template (page 36)
* scissors
* straightedges
* tape

Introduce

To reinforce your prior teaching of the Pythagorean theorem, remind students that this theorem shows the fundamental property of a perfect right angle. In addition, a right triangle includes a 90° angle and the sides can be calculated using the formula $a^2 + b^2 = c^2$. Completing this graphic organizer will help them better see the relationship among the sides of a right triangle—the square of the length of the hypotenuse equals the sum of the squares of the lengths of the other two sides.

What to Do

1. Distribute the template to students.
2. Direct students to label the following elements: right angle (90°), side a, side b, side c (hypotenuse). They should then create grids of squares on each of the vertical flaps to show the relationship among the areas of the squared sides. The smallest side will have a 3 x 3 grid, the hypotenuse (longest side) will have a 5 x 5 grid, and the mid-sized side will have a 4 x 4 grid.
3. Have students title their graphic organizers "The Pythagorean Theorem" and include the formula $a^2 + b^2 = c^2$.
4. Guide students in folding and taping the sides of the template.

How to Construct

1. Cut out the shape, as indicated.
2. Label the important information on the triangle.
3. Have students complete the grid lines on the squares to show the square units of each one.
4. Be sure to title the organizer and include the formula.
5. Fold the three square flaps up and secure them with tape.

Extend

Have students find objects in the shape of right triangles around the classroom or bring them from home. Have the students measure the sides of their triangles and apply the Pythagorean theorem to prove they are right triangles.

Ways to Use Across the Curriculum

* **Reading/Language Arts:** Explore the etymology of triangle terms.
* **Social Studies:** Record important biographical facts about Pythagoras.
* **Science:** Show examples of the importance of right triangles in engineering.

Right Triangle Template

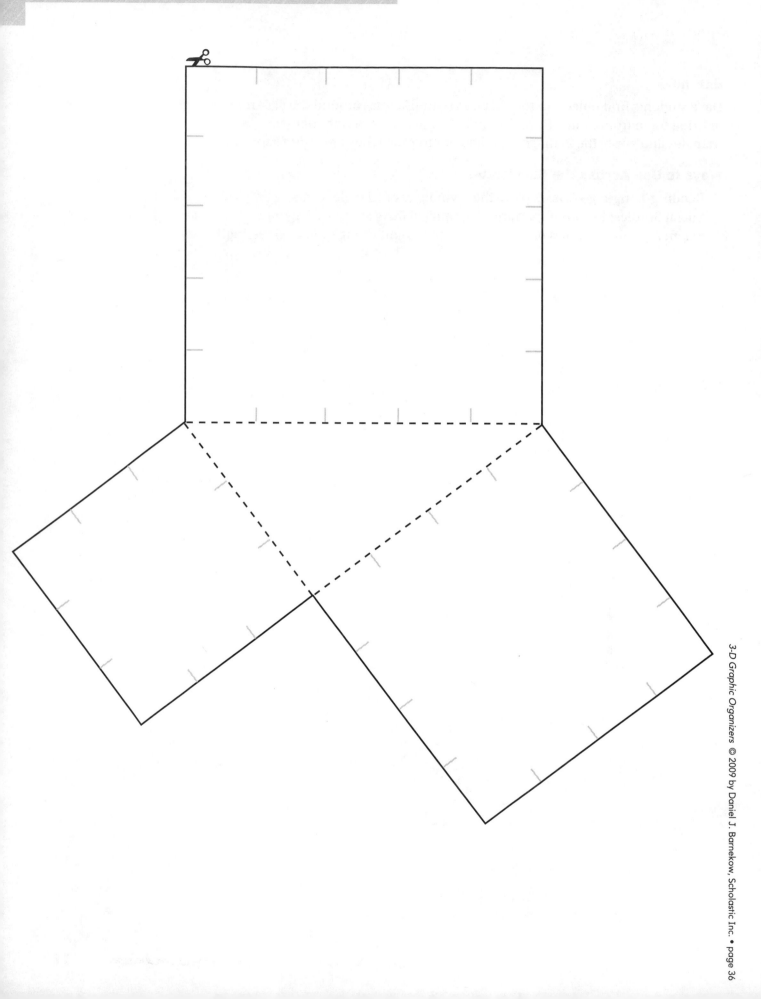

3-D Graphic Organizers © 2009 by Daniel J. Barnekow, Scholastic Inc. • page 36

Triple Flap

This 3-D graphic organizer helps students highlight key characteristics of an object and compare and contrast different objects or ideas.

Objectives

* Define igneous, sedimentary, and metamorphic rocks.
* Compare and contrast igneous, sedimentary, and metamorphic rocks.

Time Required

* about 45 minutes

Materials

* Triple Flap Template (page 39)
* scissors

Introduce

If possible, share actual examples of the three types of rocks with students. Challenge students to see if the way each rock was formed is evident in the rocks' appearance.

What to Do

1. Distribute the template to students and guide them in its construction.
2. Direct students to title their Triple Flaps "The Three Kinds of Rocks." Have them write the names of the three types of rock (igneous, sedimentary, metamorphic) on the outside of the three flaps.
3. Have students lift the flaps and write about each type of rock. Ask them to do the following:
   * Define each type by how it is formed.
   * List physical details of each type of rock.
   * Give at least two examples of each type.
   * Draw or paste pictures of examples of the rock.

How to Construct

1. Cut out the template and the flaps, along the solid lines.
2. Turn the template horizontally and fold down the flaps.
3. Fill in the important information.

Extend

If possible, divide the class into three groups and have each group bake a large cookie that represents one of the types of rocks. A "sedimentary" cookie would be layered, a "metamorphic" cookie would be a mixture with many large pieces, and an "igneous" cookie would be of roughly the same consistency throughout.

Ways to Use Across the Curriculum

* **Reading/Language Arts:** Compare and contrast literary characters.
* **Math:** Compare fractions, decimals, and percents.
* **Social Studies:** Identify the causes of a historical event and its effects; compare and contrast cultures; identify the three branches of government and describe their roles.
* **Study Skills:** Make a K-W-L chart; compare and contrast using the principle of the Venn diagram.

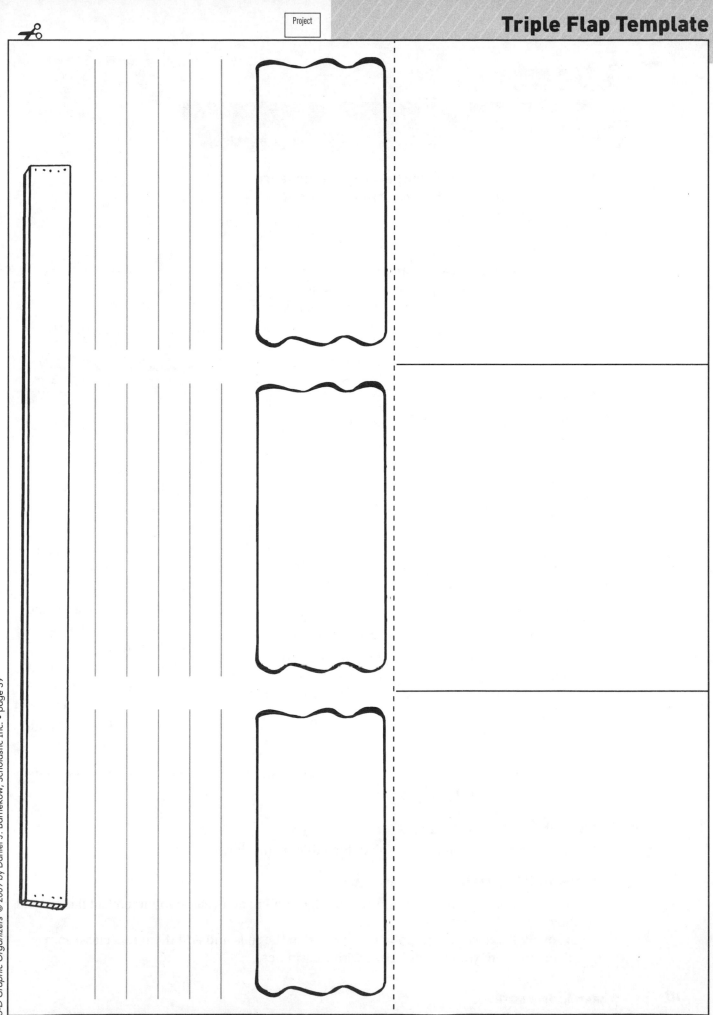

3-D Boat

This 3-D graphic organizer helps students learn and remember important information about water-related topics.

Objectives

* Collect information about an explorer.
* Demonstrate knowledge of key facts about a selected explorer's life and accomplishments.

Time Required

* about 45 minutes in addition to research time

Materials

* 3-D Boat Template (page 41)
* scissors
* tape

Introduce

Invite students to offer their ideas about why people explore, and to share any stories they'd like about places they and their families have visited that were new to them. How did they feel? Do they think that's the same way explorers of long ago might have felt?

What to Do

1. Assign, or have students choose, explorers to research.

2. Have students locate the following information: name, country of origin, country explored for, dates of voyage(s), area(s) explored, major accomplishments.

3. Distribute the template to students and guide them in its construction.

4. Have students write the name of their explorer on the large sails, and the facts they learned about them on the hull of the boat.

Extend

Create a "fleet" of graphic organizers for a tabletop display.

Ways to Use Across the Curriculum

* **Science:** Illustrate different things you might find in an ocean habitat; collect facts about the oceans or other bodies of water.
* **Study Skills:** Record your good study skills on the sails and add them to a classroom "fleet" to share your helpful ideas with classmates.

Vasco da Gama
(1460 – 1524)

- Sailed for Portugal.
- 1497 – 1498 Discovered sea route to Asia.
- Sailed around from Portugal around Africa to India.
- Set up Portuguese rule in Calicut, India

How to Construct

1. Cut out the shapes, as indicated.

2. Fill in the important information.

3. Curve and tape two halves of boat together along the bottom.

4. Fold transom and floor as indicated and tape to boat halves.

5. Tightly roll the shaded straight piece lengthwise to form mast. Tape closed.

6. Tape sail to mast and tape mast into boat.

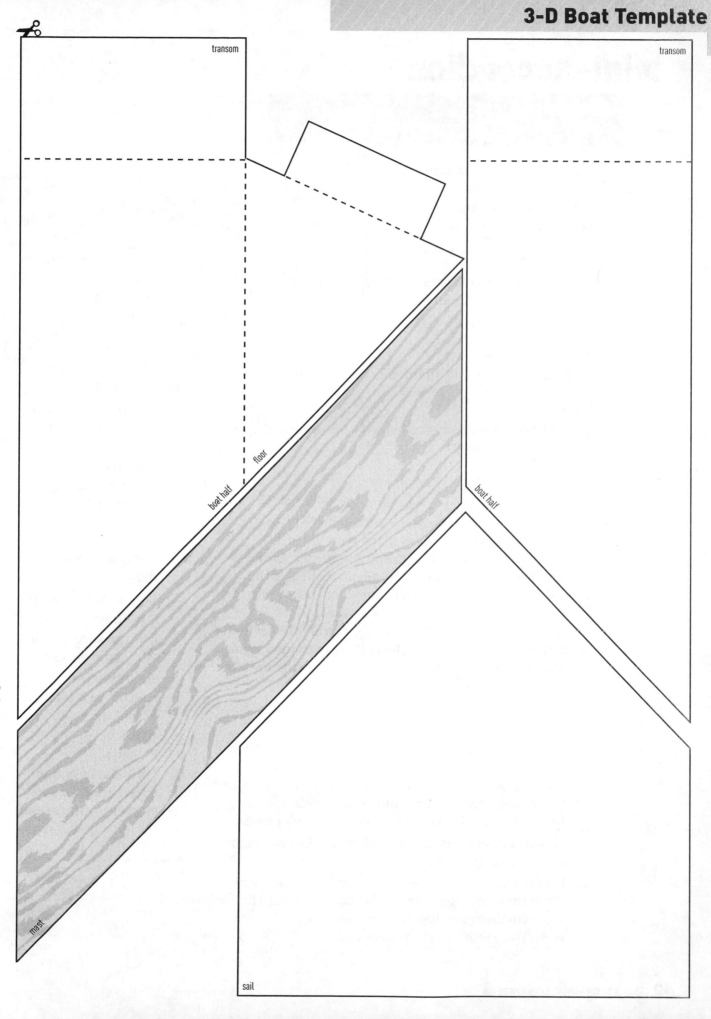

transom

transom

floor

boat half

boat half

mast

sail

Mini-Accordion

This 3-D graphic organizer provides students with a way to collect and sequence information.

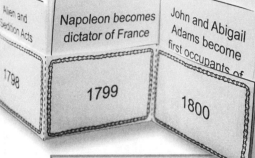

Objectives

* Identify key events (or steps).
* Place events in chronological order (or sequence).

Time Required

* about 60 minutes in addition to research time

Materials

* Mini-Accordion Template (page 44—provide multiple copies, as needed)
* scissors
* tape

Introduce

Invite students to tell you how many years are in a U.S. presidential term. *(four)* Assign one or more terms to each student. Because there are 44 presidents, with 56 terms in total, you may want to assign more than one president and/or term per student or groups of students. (Or, encourage individual students to select an additional term to complete for extra credit.) Direct them to create a mini-timeline by researching and selecting the most significant event for each of the terms.

What to Do

1. Distribute the template to students and guide them in its construction.
2. Have students write the following along the tops of the four panels: presidential number and president's name, political party, years of term, vice president's name.
3. On the four pockets, students should write each of the four years of the term.
4. On the information slips, encourage students to write down the event they think is the most important for each year. (For the incumbent president, divide the time served into four even time periods.)

How to Construct

1. Cut out the template and information slips, along the solid lines.
2. Turn the page over so the printing is facedown. Fold up the bottom panel into a long "pocket." The boxes should be showing.
3. Tape shut the ends of the pocket.
4. Fold the sheet in half so that the boxes are on the outside.
5. Fold up each side toward the center crease to create four panels.
6. Fill in the important information on the graphic organizer and the information slips.

Extend

After each term has been accounted for, have students put them in order and tape together to create a complete U.S. Presidents timeline. Display on a countertop or tack to a bulletin board. As they learn more, you may also encourage students to continue adding important events to each year's pocket.

Ways to Use Across the Curriculum

* **Reading/Language Arts:** Describe the sequence of events in a novel or chapter book; draw pictures of characters and record their traits.
* **Math:** Practice identifying the place value of whole numbers and decimals; list the four arithmetic operations and include examples of each.
* **Science:** Study the four seasons; review the four phases of the moon; create a timeline of important inventions or scientific discoveries.
* **Study Skills:** Prioritize tasks in order of importance or due date; record things to focus on in different subject areas.

Mini-Accordion Template

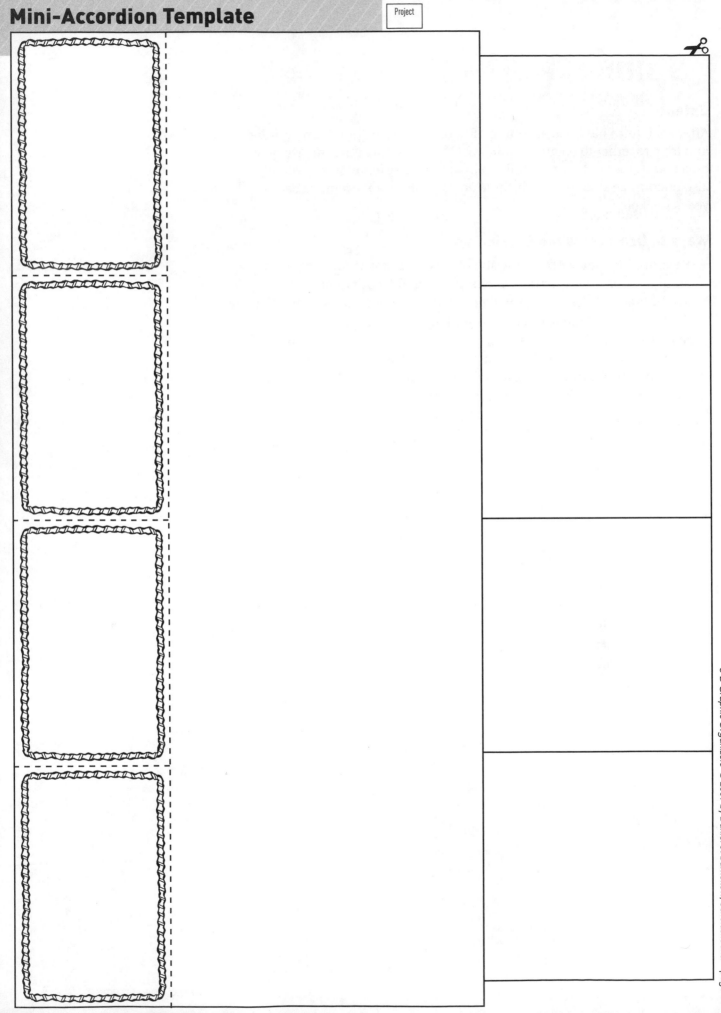

Spinning Wheel

SAMPLE PROJECT:
Math: Fractions, Decimals, and Percents

This 3-D graphic organizer helps students identify equivalent or related elements.

Objectives

* Convert among fractions, decimals, and percents.
* Memorize common fraction/decimal/percent equivalents.

Time Required

* about 75 minutes

Materials

* Spinning Wheel Template (pages 47 and 48)
* scissors
* brads (one per student)

Introduce

Ask students if they would rather have 1/4 or .25 or 25 percent of a pie. Explain how decimals, fractions, and percents can express the same value.

How to Construct

1. Cut out, as indicated.
2. Fill in important information.
3. Fasten two circles together in center with brad. The smaller circle goes on top.

What to Do

1. Distribute the template to students.
2. Have students fill in the fraction, decimal, or percent boxes on Wheel B from only *one* of the columns in the chart (below). For example, students can record percents in the boxes on the outer ring, decimals in the middle ring, and fractions in the inner ring.

Fraction	Decimal	Percent
1/10	.10	10%
1/4	.25	25%
1/3	.33	33%
1/2	.50	50%
2/3	.66	66%
3/4	.75	75%
9/10	.90	90%
1	1.0	100%

3. Guide students in constructing their graphic organizers and manipulating them.

4. Direct students to complete their graphic organizer by calculating the equivalent values and filling in the empty boxes in each row.

Extend

Pair students and have them challenge each other to correctly identify fraction, decimal, and percent equivalents.

Ways to Use Across the Curriculum

* **Reading/Language Arts:** List authors and examples of their works; practice spelling words with mnemonic devices.
* **Social Studies:** Identify map symbols and their meanings; record dates and events.
* **Science:** Display the colors of the spectrum; create a color wheel.

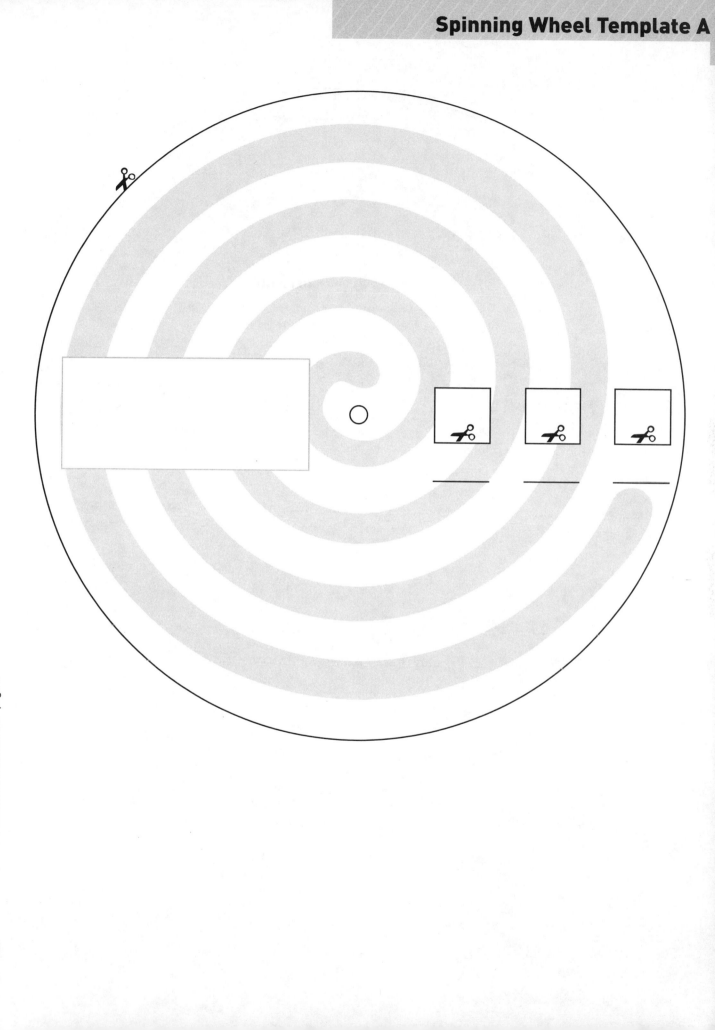

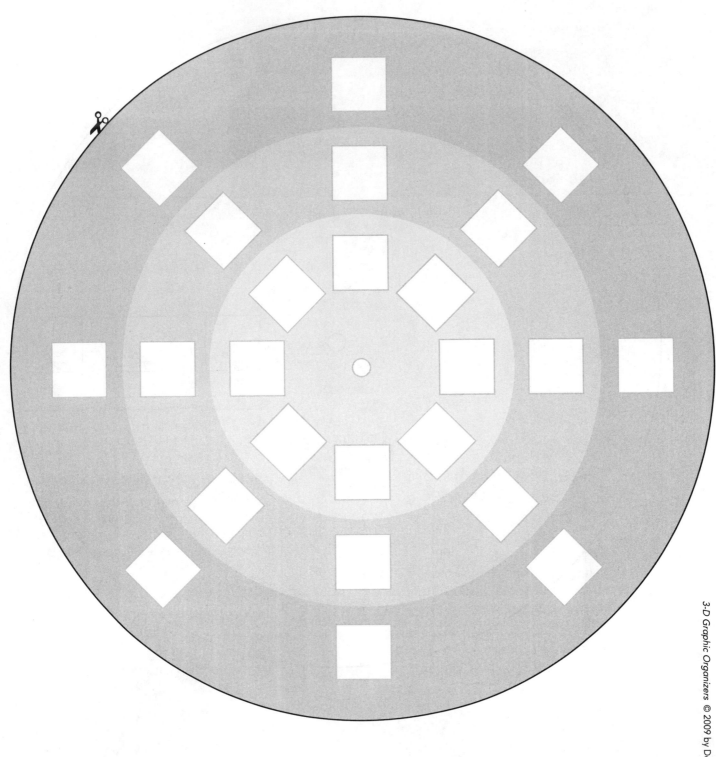

Slide Chart

This 3-D graphic organizer helps students organize and classify various types of information.

Objectives

* Define scientific classification.
* Identify each of the seven main groups in scientific classification: kingdom, phylum (or division), class, order, family, genus, and species.
* Express the relative size of each of the seven levels in scientific classification.

Time Required

* about 45 minutes

Materials

* Slide Chart Template (pages 50 and 51)
* scissors
* tape

Introduce

Ask students what a turtle is. Guide them to identify it as both an animal and a reptile. Explain how every living thing can be classified into seven groups, and define scientific classification for students.

What to Do

1. Assign, or have students choose, one animal to classify.
2. Guide students in their research to identify the classification of the animal.
3. Distribute the template to students and guide them in its construction.
4. Have students title their slide charts with the name of their animal and then write the scientific group names in the boxes on the body of the chart. On the corresponding insert, students should write the correct terms for their animal.
5. Ensure that students complete their slide charts in the proper order, so that the classification goes from large to small (i.e., kingdom, phylum [or division], class, order, family, genus, and species).

Extend

Encourage students to memorize the major divisions in scientific classification. Use completed slide charts to quiz the class. Challenge students to identify animals in each scientific group.

Ways to Use Across the Curriculum

* **Reading/Language Arts:** Distinguish parts of speech; ask and answer questions about a book.
* **Math:** Visually depict fractions, decimals, and percents.
* **Social Studies:** Name major landforms and identify their characteristics.
* **Study Skills:** Create a project timeline or checklist.

How to Construct

1. Cut out the template along the solid lines.
2. Fold as indicated.
3. Tape body closed. Tape insert closed.
4. Fill in important information.
5. Slide insert into body.

Slide Chart Template

Project

Topic:

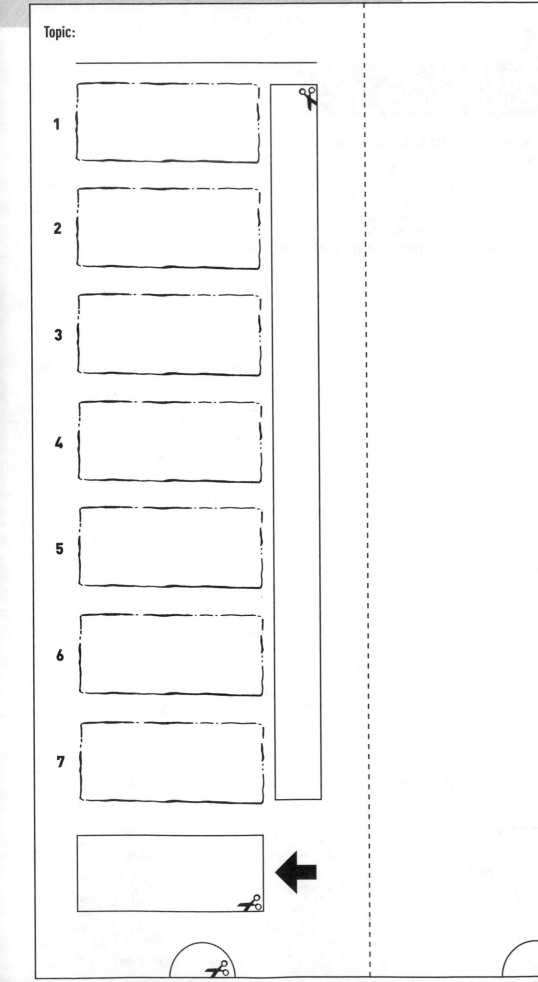

1

2

3

4

5

6

7

body

3-D Graphic Organizers © 2009 by Daniel J. Barnekow, Scholastic Inc. • page 50

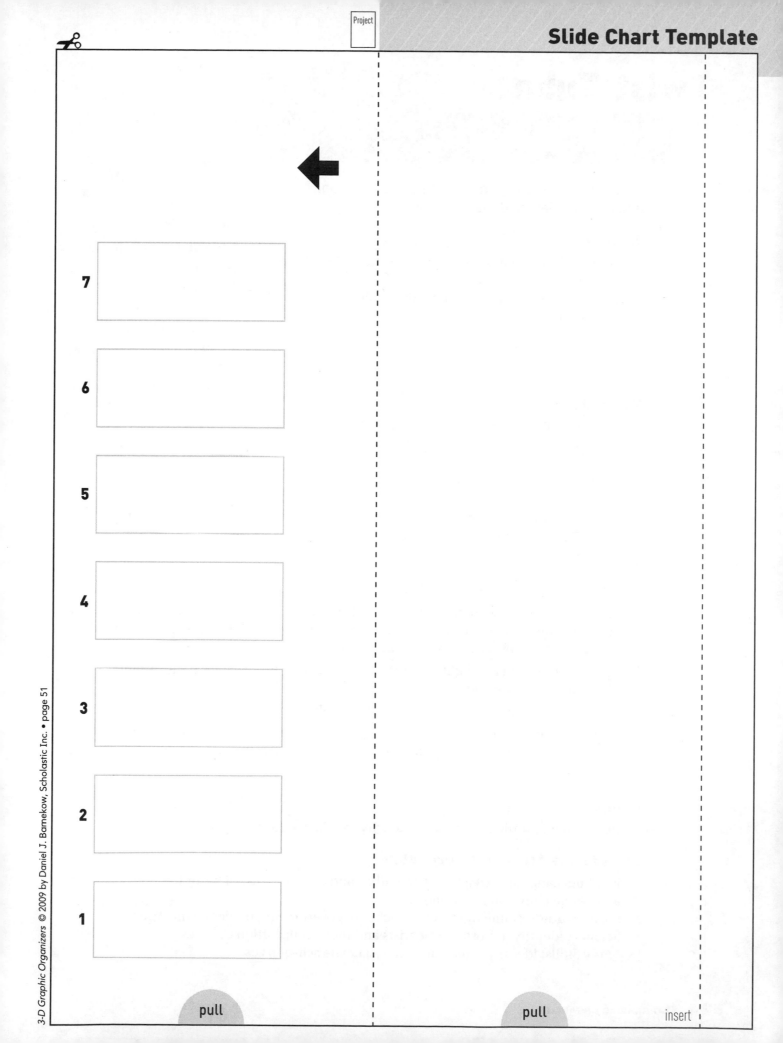

Project

Slide Chart Template

7

6

5

4

3

2

1

pull

pull

insert

Twist Tube

This 3-D graphic organizer helps students pair like or associated ideas.

Objectives

* Identify place values up to four places to the left of the decimal point.
* Explain the relationship among place values in the base ten system.

Time Required

* about 30 minutes

Materials

* Twist Tube Template (pages 53 and 54)
* scissors
* tape

How to Construct

1. Cut out, as indicated.
2. Fill in important information.
3. Roll body lengthwise and tape closed.
4. Roll insert lengthwise and tape closed. Cut and fold up tabs on insert to create "handles."

Introduce

Challenge students to come up with real-life situations in which knowing the different place values is important (for example, in making change).

What to Do

1. Distribute the template to students.
2. Direct students to write the numeral 1,000 in row 1, column 1 of the insert with the last zero highlighted in some way, such as in red or underlined. Students should write the word "ones" in row 1, column 2 of the insert.
3. Guide students in highlighting and naming the other place values (tens through thousands) in remaining spaces.
4. Guide students in the construction of the graphic organizer.
5. Have students operate their graphic organizers and work on memorizing place values. Remind them that with each jump to the left of the ones place, the place value increases by ten.

Extend

Using alternate numbers, repeat the activity for place values.

Ways to Use Across the Curriculum

* **Reading/Language Arts:** Select an author and compile a list of his or her books; identify and define common homophones.
* **Social Studies:** Name the three branches of government and define their purpose.
* **Science:** Identify important scientists and their contributions.
* **Study Skills:** Identify causes and effects; create self-quizzes.

Project

body

tape edge here

Insert tube from this direction

Twist Tube Template

Project

Row 4

Row 3

Row 2

Row 1

Column 1

insert

Column 2

tape edge here

Double Twist Tube

This 3-D graphic organizer helps students pair like or associated ideas.

Objectives

* Identify synonyms of a target word.
* Identify antonyms of a target word.

Time Required

* about 30 minutes

Materials

* Double Twist Tube Template (pages 56 and 57)
* scissors
* tape

Introduce

Write the words "synonyms" and "antonyms" on the board and explain what they mean. Invite students to provide examples of each for several common words such as *good*, *small*, and *friendly*.

What to Do

1. Assign a target word to each student.
2. Distribute the template to students.
3. Direct students to write their assigned word on the line between the two windows on the body. They then write antonyms of the word in the boxes on the left insert and synonyms of the word in the boxes on the right insert.
4. Guide students in the construction the template.
5. Have students use their Double Twist Tubes to memorize the synonyms and antonyms of their target words.

Extend

Have students quiz each other on the synonyms and antonyms of their words; have students exchange their organizers to learn the synonyms and antonyms of other students' words.

Ways to Use Across the Curriculum

* **Math:** Match equivalent fractions, decimals, and percents
* **Social Studies:** Match U.S. presidents to their terms in office
* **Science:** Match planets with their characteristics
* **Study Skills:** Create self-quizzes

How to Construct

1. Cut out, as indicated.
2. Fill in important information.
3. Roll body and tape closed.
4. Roll both inserts and tape closed. Cut and fold up tabs on inserts to create "handles."

Double Twist Tube Template

tape edge here

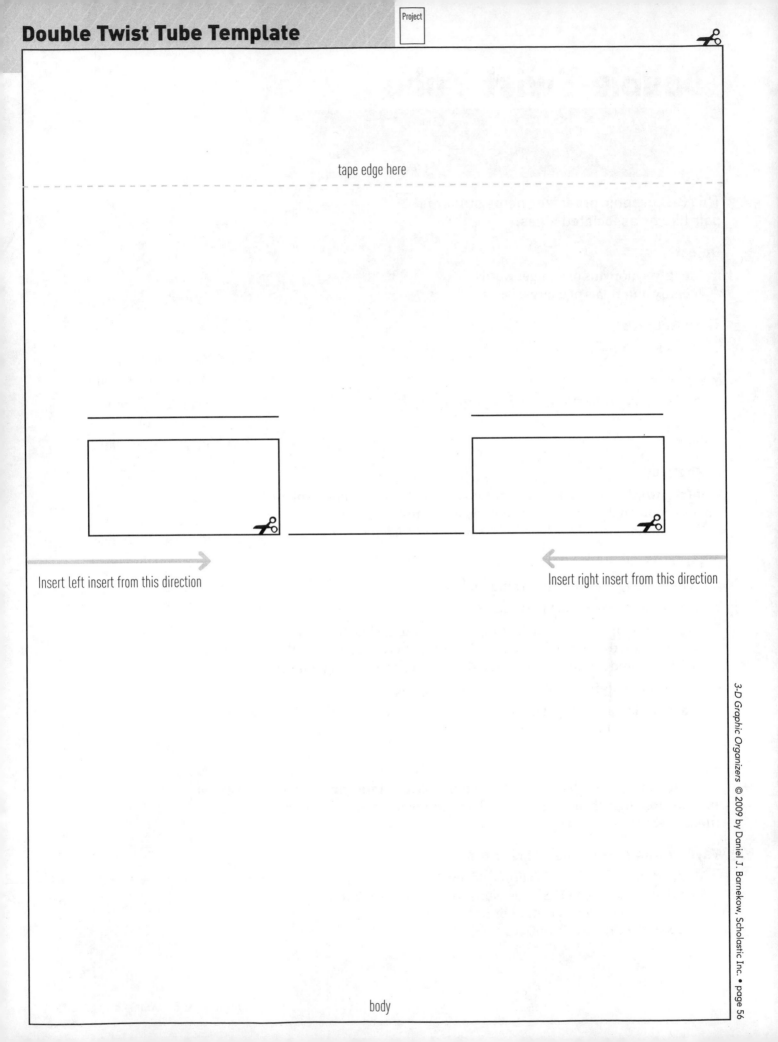

Insert left insert from this direction

Insert right insert from this direction

body

Project

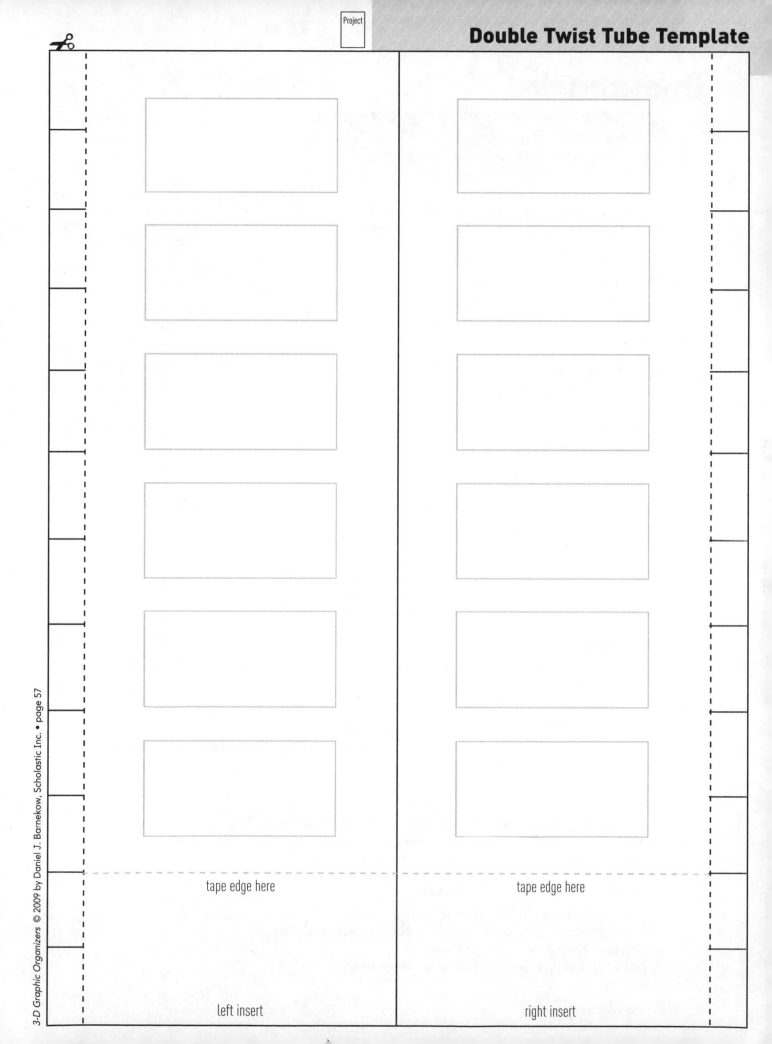

Double Twist Tube Template

tape edge here

tape edge here

left insert

right insert

Bookmark

Students create a bookmark that acts as a place to note unfamiliar words or concepts.

Objectives

* Read actively.
* Recognize unfamiliar words as such.
* Use context clues and a dictionary to determine the meanings of words.

Time Required

* about 15 minutes for instruction and construction

Materials

* Bookmark Template (page 59)
* scissors
* double-sided tape

Introduce

Ask students what they should do when they come across a word they don't know. Remind them of the options they have (using context clues, consulting a dictionary, asking other readers, and so on). Explain that they will make bookmarks on which they should note any unfamiliar words they encounter while reading.

What to Do

1. Distribute the template to students and guide them in its construction.

2. Direct students to use the bookmark as a place to write down any unfamiliar words and the page numbers on which each word first appears.

3. Help students to determine the meanings of the words by using context clues and/or a dictionary.

Extend

Have students "teach" their classmates one of the new words on their bookmarks. Have them each read their word in context and then explain its meaning to the class. Provide additional templates to students to use throughout the year.

Ways to Use Across the Curriculum

* **Math:** Note formulas or tips and hints.
* **Social Studies:** Note key vocabulary, people, places, and dates.
* **Science:** Note new scientific terms.
* **Study Skills:** Take notes for all types of reading.

How to Construct

1. Cut out the template, cut along solid lines.

2. Fold page in half from left to right. Make a hard crease.

3. Fold page in half from top to bottom. Make a hard crease.

4. Open the top flap and tape, as indicated.

5. The inside pocket of the bookmark slips over the top corner of the left-hand page, creating a "pad" for notetaking.

tape here

tape here

Mobile 1

Students make mobiles that display
the definition of a topic and include
key examples or details.

Objectives

* Define a selected part of speech.
* Identify examples of a selected part of speech.

Time Required

* about 30 minutes

Materials

* Mobile 1 Template (page 61)
* scissors
* tape
* hole punch
* string

Introduce

Remind students of the eight parts of speech (nouns,
verbs, adjectives, adverbs, pronouns, interjections,
conjunctions, and prepositions). Each student will work
with one of them.

How to Construct

1. Cut out, as indicated.
2. Punch out holes.
3. Attach smaller pieces to large piece with tape and string.
4. Fill in important information.

What to Do

1. Invite students to choose or assign one part of speech to each student.
2. Distribute the template to students and guide them in its construction.
3. Students label the main section of the mobile with the name of their part of speech and write its definition. On the smaller sections, they provide several examples of the part of speech.

Extend

Hang mobiles in the classroom and leave them up as reinforcement.

Ways to Use Across the Curriculum

* **Math:** Collect formulas; describe arithmetic operations.
* **Social Studies:** Record facts about a community, state, or country.
* **Science:** Identify examples of a landform; describe traits of an animal; record details about planets in our solar system.
* **Study Skills:** Keep track of good communication skills, key classroom rules, and effective study skills.

Mobile 2

Students construct mobiles to help them learn and remember the appearance, names, and characteristics of objects.

Objectives

* Recognize and name a variety of flat shapes.
* Identify key characteristics of flat shapes.

Time Required

* about 30 minutes

Materials

* Mobile 2 Template (pages 63 and 64)
* scissors
* tape
* hole punch
* string

Introduce

Invite students to locate and identify as many shapes in the classroom as they can.

What to Do

1. Distribute the template to students and guide them in its construction.
2. Have students label the main section of the mobile "Flat Shapes" (or "Two-Dimensional Shapes") and label the smaller shapes with the appropriate names.
3. You might choose to have students identify the characteristics of the shapes on the reverse side of each one.

Extend

Hang the mobiles in the classroom and leave them up as reinforcement.

How to Construct

1. Cut out, as indicated.
2. Punch out holes.
3. Secure smaller pieces to large piece with tape and string.
4. Fill in important information.

Ways to Use Across the Curriculum

* **Reading/Language Arts:** Select and define unfamiliar vocabulary words from a single text; identify one trait of a character in a book and provide examples from the text to support the choice.
* **Social Studies:** Choose a famous historical figure and list some of their important accomplishments; identify a place and describe six of its characteristics.
* **Science:** Gather facts about different weather phenomena; show the relationship between U.S. and metric measurements.
* **Study Skills:** Brainstorm and write about six study habits and why they are effective.

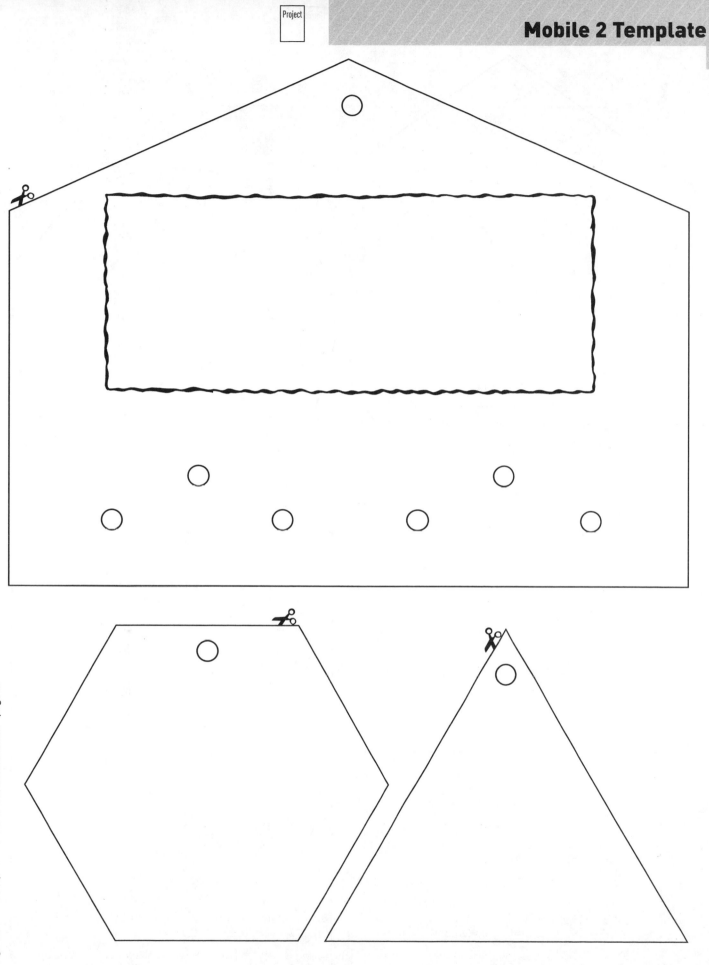

Project

Mobile 2 Template

Project

Mobile 2 Template

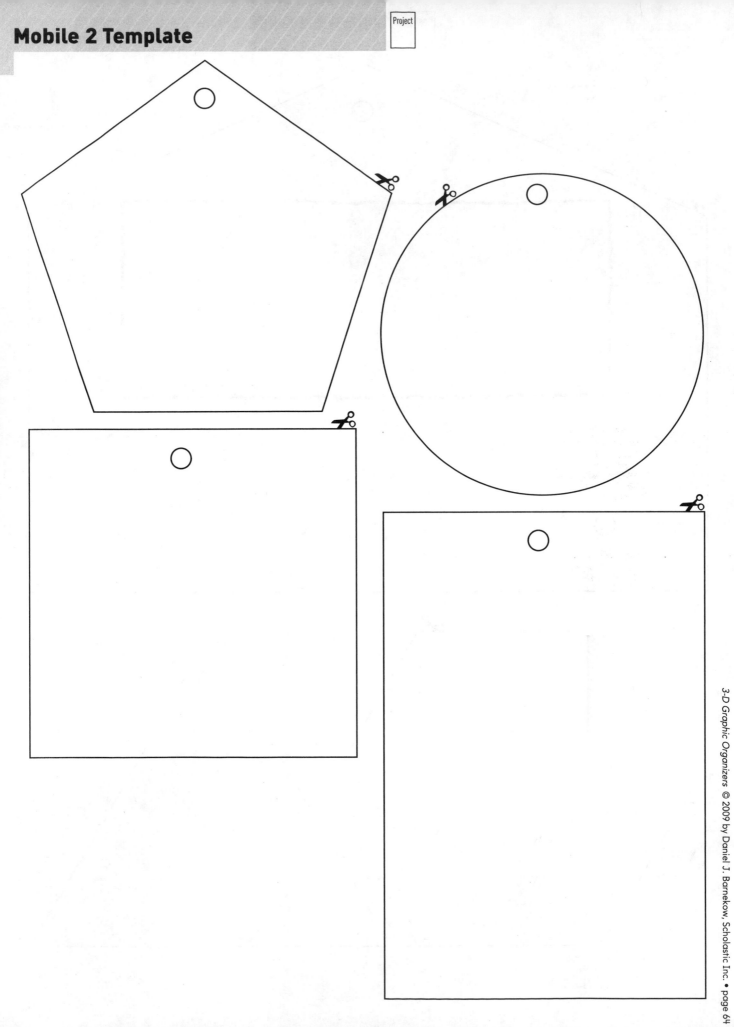